# The Earth and the Universe

## How the Sun, Moon, and Stars Cause Changes on Earth

ABC CHARTER SCHOOL

The aim of this book is to present to children an explanation of natural phenomena and human activities related to astronomy and the universe. During a great summer vacation, our main characters become interested in and understand many mysteries of the world—tides, lunar phases, seasons of the year. The enclosed teaching guidelines and a simple practical exercise are the ideal complements for young and old to understand the physics of the universe.

English translation of *The Earth and the Universe*
©Copyright 1998 by Barron's Educational Series, Inc.

©Copyright TREVOL PRODUCCIONS EDITORIALS S.C.P., 1998. Barcelona, Spain.

Original title of the book in Catalan: *La Terra i l'Univers; la influència de l'Univers a la Terra.*

*Address all inquiries to:*
Barron's Educational Series, Inc.
250 Wireless Boulevard
Hauppauge, New York 11788
http://www.barronseduc.com


International Standard Book Number 0-7641-0687-2

Library of Congress Catalog Card Number 98-73388


Printed in Spain


987654321

# The Earth and the Universe

## How the Sun, Moon, and Stars
## Cause Changes on Earth

Text: Miquel Pérez  Illustrations: Maria Rius

BARRON'S

It is an old tradition for people to celebrate the arrival of summer, good weather, and harvest time. In the northern countries of the Earth, June 21st marks the end of spring. It is the day in which people celebrate the summer solstice, the longest day of the year. However, for people living in the southern countries of our planet, this day represents the shortest day and the end of autumn.

For northern children the days will grow shorter from now on, until the winter solstice occurs on December 22nd and they have the shortest day of the year. The Earth will have made a complete turn around the sun and a full year will have passed. But for the kids living in the south December 22nd will be the longest day, just a few days away from a hot, sunny Christmas!

I have started my vacation notebook and have illustrated the explanation the teacher gave us at school about the four seasons of the year and the rotation of the Earth around the sun. Do you have your notebook?

It is our summer vacation. My family is taking a long camping trip.

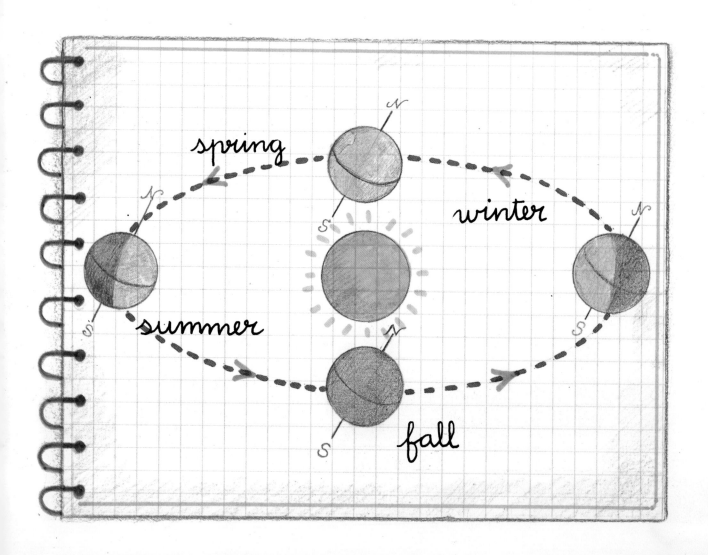

After a long journey, we got up early this morning to go to the bakery and, what a surprise! The town clock indicated two hours less than our watches did. Our parents told us that this time difference is due to the fact that we traveled, following the sun, from east to west. That's why the sun sets two hours later here. In our notebooks we have written that the Earth takes a day to turn around itself and, as it does, the sun illuminates different areas on its surface. When the area we are in is illuminated by the sun, we are in daylight; on the other side of the Earth it is night.

Now we are exploring near our campsite. Look! Plants grow here, in the middle of these rocks with almost no soil, and there were no plants growing inside the dark cave. Our parents have explained that plants cannot live without light from the sun because it is their main source of energy. Plants absorb the sun's rays and use the energy to make substances necessary for life. Through this process, plants free into the atmosphere the oxygen we need to breathe. The sun is life.

The moon looks different every night, because different parts of its surface reflect sunlight to us. These differences are called *lunar phases* and they are repeated every 29½ days. During this cycle, one half of the moon is always illuminated by the sun, but we can see the entire moon on one night when there is a *full moon* and it looks like an O. When it looks like a D, it is a *waxing crescent moon* or first quarter. When it looks like a C, it is a *waning crescent moon* or last quarter. When we can hardly see it, it is a *new moon*.

Tonight we were lucky enough to observe a lunar (moon) eclipse. This astronomical event occurs only when the Earth gets between the sun and the moon. On these occasions we can see how the shadow of our planet slowly covers our satellite; the moon does not actually disappear completely but what we see of it is much darker.

When the moon passes in front of the sun and obscures it, we have a solar (sun) eclipse.

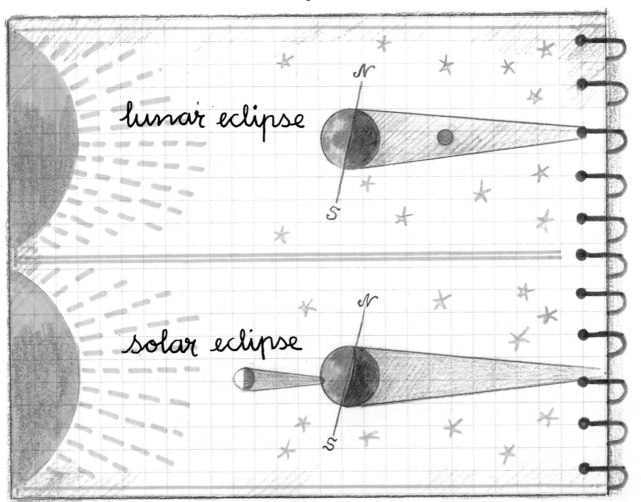

lunar eclipse

solar eclipse

Today we observed the rising and falling of the sea. This morning we walked on the sand and reached those rocks, but now we could not get there unless we swam. The gravitational attraction of the moon, and also the sun—but to a lesser extent—makes the water level of the oceans rise or fall, a phenomenon we call *tides*.

One night we saw a comet. Comets are huge dirty snowballs a few miles wide. Their orbits may approach the sun and, as they get closer, the ice starts to melt and a long tail of gas and dust is produced.

There is a Christian legend that the Three Wise Men who came from the Orient to worship the baby Jesus followed a comet that showed them the way. It is called the Star of the Magi.

While we were traveling, we talked about the Earth and the universe. From the time of the Babylonians and Egyptians, we have tried to understand the universe, but the Greeks were the first to try to explain it without referring to the supernatural. The theories of the philosopher Aristotle, and later those of the remarkable

astronomer Ptolemy, who argued that the Earth was the center of the universe, dominated the world of astronomy for fifteen centuries.

Copernicus and Galileo replaced the old concepts of the cosmos and described many features of the solar system as we know it today.

To finish our vacation notebook, we visited the science museum. In the room devoted to the exploration of the moon, there was a replica of the huge *Saturn V* rocket, the one that Armstrong, Aldrin and Collins used when they flew to the moon.

Once they were on the moon, Armstrong and Aldrin could see there were no plants, no oxygen, the nights were freezing, and the days scorching. The men had fun anyway, because the low gravity of the moon allowed them to jump high with little effort. In subsequent *Apollo* missions, other astronauts took pictures, gathered samples of rocks and dust, and even explored on board a lunar vehicle.

Now let's visit the exhibition of the spacecraft that has been used to explore the solar system. The *Voyager* probes have sent data and pictures of Jupiter, Saturn, Uranus, and Neptune, and we keep getting information even though they have gone beyond Pluto's orbit.

The exhibition also includes some satellites. They are devices that have no crew and that scientists launch into space in order to capture and convey images while they are flying around the Earth. Some satellites are used to transmit radio and television signals; others, like Meteosat, are very useful to meteorologists. The Hubble is a magnificent telescope that orbits so high above the atmosphere that there are no clouds to interfere with its clear observation of the universe.

With this computer and through the Internet, we can communicate with the crew of the Mir space station. Mir is a huge space laboratory that revolves around the Earth while the crew conducts scientific experiments to study the behavior of humans, animals, and plants in the absence of gravity.

"Look, now they tell us that the Mir space station is obsolete and will soon be replaced by the new Alpha station."

Would you like to take a virtual trip? Let's visit the future bases on the moon through this computer.

It's been fun and easy to fill this notebook with the many experiences we've had in the past few days. We will continue to keep our eyes open on our little planet, the Earth, to observe and understand how the universe works.

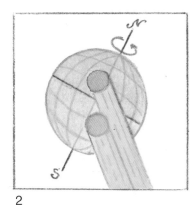

1

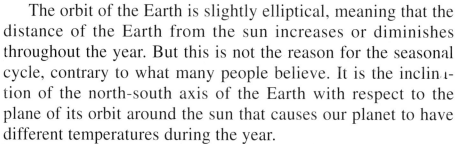

2

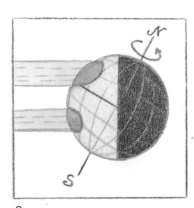

3

# Teaching Guidelines

It is not easy to understand the consequences of the movements of the Earth, the moon, and the sun in space. We are all familiar with the seasons of the year, the lunar phases, eclipses, and tides, but we do not really know how to explain them. This guideline is intended to help you clarify your ideas about these natural phenomena.

## The seasons of the year

The orbit of the Earth is slightly elliptical, meaning that the distance of the Earth from the sun increases or diminishes throughout the year. But this is not the reason for the seasonal cycle, contrary to what many people believe. It is the inclination of the north-south axis of the Earth with respect to the plane of its orbit around the sun that causes our planet to have different temperatures during the year.

On June 21st, due to this inclination, the sun's rays fall perpendicular to the Tropic of Cancer in the Northern Hemisphere. At the Tropic of Capricorn, in the Southern Hemisphere, the sun's rays are very slanted (see Figure 1). That's why in the Northern Hemisphere the sun is very high at noon, while it is quite a bit lower in the South. Thus, in the Northern Hemisphere, a ray of sun must heat a much smaller area of the Earth's surface than in the South. It is quite evident that in the former case it is summer and in the latter case it is winter. Another explanation for the increased difference in temperature between the two hemispheres is that in the Northern Hemisphere in summer, daytime is much longer than nighttime and therefore there are more hours of sunshine.

In spring and fall, at equal latitudes, both the Northern and Southern Hemispheres have the same amount of hours of light, because both daytime and nighttime last 12 hours each (see

Figure 2).The situation is different in the Southern Hemisphere. Compare all of the above with Figure 3, which shows summer in the Southern Hemisphere. The sun never sets in Antarctica on December 22nd and daytime is 24 hours long, while the opposite is true at the North Pole. Finally, in the areas close to the equator the differences between day and night in winter, spring, summer, and fall are so minimal that we can say there is virtually no variation in temperature; that is to say, they have no seasons.

## The lunar phases and eclipses

To understand the lunar phases we must know that the moon takes about 27 days to make a complete turn around the Earth (see Figure 4), that the plane of its orbit is not parallel to the plane of our orbit but is slightly inclined (see Figure 5), and the Earth and the moon are both moving in relation to the sun. Consequently, although the moon always has an illuminated face, we see varying amounts of this face on different days.

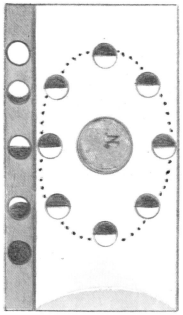

4

- when the moon passes the night side of the Earth, it usually passes above or under the shadow cone that the Earth projects into space. This is the case when there ⌐ full moon, as it is on the side exactly opposite to the sun. Sometimes, though, due to the variations in the orbit of the moon, the orbits of the moon and the Earth coincide on the same plane. If there is a full moon, then the shadow of the Earth will cover the moon, the sun's rays will not reach its surface, and the moon will grow dark. We will be watching a lunar eclipse.

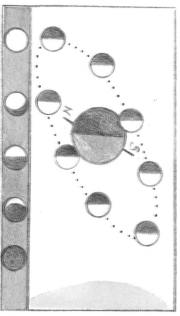

5

- when the moon is on one side of the Earth, that is, in the area that marks the limit between day and night, the moon is in the first quarter. It comes out in midafternoon and disappears at midnight, although we may not see it because of the sunlight.
- when the moon passes between the Earth and the sun, it usually does so above or under the latter. Thus, the small shadow cone projected by the moon does not reach the Earth; that is, it does not cover the sun and there is a new moon. Were it not for the glaring light of the sun, we could see it during the day. The variations in the orbit of the moon sometimes place it between the Earth and the sun; this sometimes happens when there is a new moon. The small shadow cone projected by the moon reaches a specific part of the surface of the Earth, where a solar eclipse can be observed.
- when the moon is on one side of the Earth, that is, in the area limiting night and day, the moon is in the last quarter. It comes out at midnight and it does not disappear until noon, if the rays of the sun allow us to see it.

**The tides**

This refers to the alternate cyclical movement of rising and falling of the surface of the oceans caused by the gravitational attraction of the moon and, to a lesser extent, the Sun (see Figure 8). The full cycle is formed by two rising or *flooding tides* and two falling or *ebbing tides*. When the water reaches the highest level, it is high tide; when the level is the lowest, it is low tide. The difference between these two levels of water is called *tidal range*. In lakes or inland waters, like the Mediterranean Sea, the amplitude is so small that they are generally said to have no tides.

The most spectacular cases are when the moon is new or full, because then its gravitational effect is highest. Added

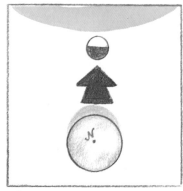

6

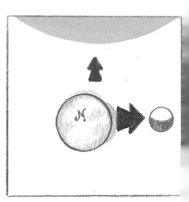

7

8

to that of the sun and working together in the same direction, the resulting tide is big and there is a *spring tide* (see Figure 6). On the other hand, when the moon is in the first or last quarter and both the moon and sun are in quadrature (90° separation), their gravitational attractions are perpendicular and the amplitude of the tide is remarkably smaller. This is called *reap tide* (see Figure 7).

## Teaching Activity

Telescopes are used to observe very large celestial bodies that are very far away. With the help of a simple telescope that we can make ourselves, we will be able to watch in more detail many of the characteristics of the sky that are so difficult to see with the naked eye. The denomination *refractor telescope* is commonly used when the principal focusing element of the light rays is a lens. It is called *reflector* when the principal focusing element is a mirror.

This practical exercise suggests the construction of a small astronomical telescope. The required materials are simple (see Figure 9) and so is its assembly.

The optical system of our telescope is formed by two lenses:

- An objective lens that forms a real image, inverted and much smaller than the object being observed, but much closer. You should use a convex-concave lens, such as ones used for presbyopia or hyperopia and which are found in eyeglasses that correct farsightedness.
- An ocular lens that is used like a regular magnifying glass to observe the image supplied by the objective lens. It is a divergent lens, like the ones used for myopia and which are found in eyeglasses that correct nearsightedness. The bigger the lenses, the better and clearer the image will be. It is difficult to indicate the exact distance that must separate these two kinds of lenses, but it can be estimated.

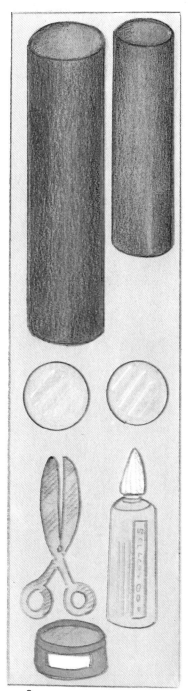

Hold the objective lens vertically and look at it through the ocular lens, moving it backward until the vision is clear. Then, measure the distance between both lenses.

The body of our telescope (see Figure 10) will be formed by two cardboard tubes, A and B, made out of two sheets of not-too-thick, flexible cardboard. In the drawing, the outer tube is A. Use flat black paint for the inside of both tubes.

- Inside tube A there is the objective lens. The inside diameter of this tube must then correspond to the diameter of the lens. If this is 2 inches (50 mm) in diameter, a 20-inch-long (50 cm) tube will be enough. Two rings, each 1.2 inches (3 cm) long glued inside the tube, will fix the lens to one end of the tube. You can also use silicone to facilitate the same effect.
- If the ocular lens is about 1.6 inches (40 mm) wide in diameter, tube B should be 9.8 inches (25 cm) long and its diameter slightly less than that of A, so that tube B can fit into tube A and slide easily forward and backward. To avoid B coming out of or going too far into A, we can glue on cardboard ends. The ocular lens must be placed in a 1.6-inch-long (4-cm-long) piece cut from the same tube B and fixed with a little bit of silicone. Slightly reduce the diameter of this piece so it can fit inside the tube.

10

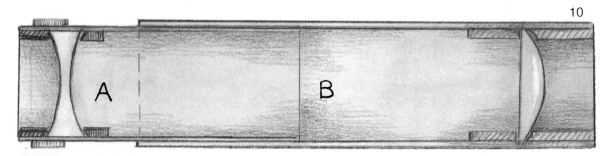

Enjoy your telescope and, if you are very interested in astronomy, you can buy better lenses or even a complete telescopic kit.

ABC CHARTER SCHOOL